D1624864

Bible to Go

Bible to Go

GENESIS TO REVELATION
IN ONE HOUR

Stan Campbell

NEW YORK   BOSTON   NASHVILLE

FaithWords
Hachette Book Group USA
237 Park Avenue
New York, NY 10169

Visit our Web site at www.faithwords.com.

Printed in the United States of America

Book Design by Paula Russell Szafranski

Previously published by Viking Canada in 2006.

First FaithWords Edition: August 2007

10 9 8 7 6 5 4 3 2 1

The FaithWords name and logo are trademarks of Hachette Book Group USA.

Library of Congress Cataloging-in-Publication Data

Campbell, Stan
  Bible to go : Genesis to Revelation in one hour / Stan Campbell. — 1st Faith Words ed.
    p. cm.
  Summary: "A compilation of overviews of each book of the Bible for people who have an interest in Christianity but not the time to read the whole Bible." — Provided by the publisher.
  ISBN-13: 978-0-446-58051-9
  ISBN-10: 0-446-58051-1
  1. Bible — Introductions. I. Title.
  BS475.3.C355 2007
  220.6'1 — dc22   2006022973

Contents

INTRODUCTION

The *Bible to Go: Genesis to Revelation in One Hour*. You've picked up the book, but you're still wondering, *What does "to go" mean?*

First, it is my intent with this book to help people who may be unfamiliar with the Bible to accumulate a working knowledge of its contents—from Genesis to Revelation—in a short time. I know you're busy and may not have time to devote to extensive reading or study. And even if you do, when it comes to the Bible, it can be difficult to know how and where to begin. So if you're continually on the go, this book can go with you and provide a quick yet meaningful introduction of what is in the Bible.

Also, when you think of the title *Bible to Go,* it's a reminder that the Bible is not an old, outdated, irrelevant book. It is a book of action, of motion, of life. The author of Hebrews says, "The word of God is living and active" (Hebrews 4:12), and many people today will attest to that statement.

Woven throughout the Bible is a story line, a plot, a flow of action. The *Bible to Go* will follow that motion from start to finish. We won't be able to go in-depth. Yet I hope what is here will be beneficial to you, moving you to a better understanding of the Bible, and maybe even a more personal interest and desire to apply what you're learning.

So, on your mark. Get set. Let's go!

Bible to Go

ONE

Beginnings

It's always good to start at the beginning, yet at the beginning of the Bible we find God already present (Genesis 1:1). The theological belief that God is eternal means not only that he will exist forever into the future but also that he has always existed into the eternity of the past.

Creation (GENESIS 1–2)

You'll notice that it's completely dark as we begin our journey through the Bible. We're also in a place that is formless and empty. But all it takes is a word from God and immediately there is light. Another word, and the sky and earth separate. A few more words, and the new world is teeming with plants, animals, and the first human beings (see pages 97–98). After each day of

Creation, God declares his work "good." After humankind is established, however, God evaluates all he has
done and deems it "very good" (Genesis 1:31).

Adam and Eve (GENESIS 2:15–3:24)

Adam, the first created human, is assigned the task
of naming all the animals. In doing so, he notices that
for him there is "no suitable helper" (Genesis 2:20), so
God places him in a deep sleep and uses one of his ribs
to create Eve. God places them in the Garden of Eden,
naked but without shame.

Eden is a paradise. But in time, Adam and Eve do
the one thing God has instructed them not to do.
After being tempted by a serpent, they succumb and
eat of the fruit of the tree of the knowledge of good
and evil. As a result, they recognize their nakedness
and hide from God.

This "original sin" initiates a separation from God
that has made it more difficult for humans to interact
with him throughout the centuries. It results, too, in
a curse on the serpent, on Adam (thorns, thistles, and
sweat as impediments to future work) and Eve (pain
in childbirth and subjection to her husband). But it
also results in the Bible's first messianic prophecy: a
time will come when a descendant of Adam and Eve
(Jesus) will "crush the head" of the serpent (Satan),

even though the serpent will "strike his heel" (Genesis 3:14–19).

Cain and Abel (GENESIS 4:1–16)

After Adam and Eve are evicted from Eden (to prevent their eating from the tree of life and living forever in a state of separation from God), it doesn't take long for sin to spread. When God rejects an offering from their older son, Cain, and accepts one from their younger son, Abel, Cain responds in a fit of jealousy. He lures Abel into a field and commits the first premeditated murder. When questioned by God, he tries to plead ignorance—to no avail.

Early Personalities (GENESIS 4:17–5:32)

Soon afterward we come to Lamech, who was the first known polygamist, and boastful as well. But we also read of the first rancher (Jabal), musician (Jubal), and metalworker (Tubal-Cain). And this is where we find the Bible's oldest character: Methuselah, who lives to be 969 years old. With such age spans, it's no surprise that people are fruitful and multiply, and the population grows.

But so does sin. People live and die and generally ignore God. Yet a couple of people stand out as positive examples. One is Enoch, the father of Methuselah. We are told, "Enoch walked with God; then he was no more, because God took him away" (Genesis 5:24). This cryptic statement is better explained in Hebrews 11:5, which tells us that because Enoch pleased God, God didn't require that Enoch face physical death.

Noah (GENESIS 6–9)

Another exception is Noah, who "was a righteous man, blameless among the people of his time, and he walked with God" (Genesis 6:9). Sin has finally reached the point where "the LORD was grieved that he had made man on the earth, and his heart was filled with pain" (Genesis 6:6). At this time, God limits human life spans to 120 years (Genesis 6:3). He also tells Noah to build a three-deck ark in anticipation of a devastating flood. The ark is to be 450 feet long, 75 feet wide, and 45 feet high. By the time he finishes it, Noah is six hundred years old. Two of every kind of bird and animal come to him, and he boards them along with seven pairs of clean (kosher) animals and birds, which can be used for food and later, for sacrifices. Then God shuts the animals and eight people (Noah, his wife, his three sons, and their wives) in the ark.

The rain begins to fall, and the waters also rise up from "all the springs of the great deep" (Genesis 7:11). After forty days, the earth is covered. It takes time for the waters to recede, however. Noah and his family are in the ark for just over a year before a dove indicates the land is dry enough for them to disembark (Genesis 7:11, 8:13–14). It is at this point that God provides the rainbow as a sign of the covenant he makes with Noah to never again destroy the earth with a flood (Genesis 9:11–17).

And although God has given humankind a second chance to eliminate the wickedness that had become so rampant, it doesn't take long for sin to return. Noah plants a vineyard, gets drunk, gets naked, and is observed by one of his sons, who ridicules him. When he discovers his son's insult, he places a curse on that son's descendants (who will become the Canaanites).

The Tower of Babel (GENESIS 11:1–9)

And the next major story we come to is of the Tower of Babel, where a community of people are determined to build a tower into the heavens in order to "make a name for ourselves" (Genesis 11:4), and ostensibly, to share God's glory. But God "confused their language" (Genesis 11:7) so they can no longer communicate with one another, and they scatter to various parts of the world.

So although we've only just begun our journey through the Bible, it's already filled with action. And from here, the pace just picks up. Next comes the era of the patriarchs.

TWO

The Patriarchs

From Mesopotamia to Israel

So far, the action of the Bible has taken place in the "fertile crescent" of the Middle East. The Garden of Eden was located near the confluence of the Tigris and Euphrates rivers (Genesis 2:10–14). Noah's ark came to rest on Mount Ararat (Genesis 8:4), believed to be in what is now Turkey. The city of Babylon (in modern Iraq) has already been established and the Tower of Babel was nearby. So when does the action of the Bible shift to the land of Israel? Right now.

Abraham (GENESIS 12–23)

A resident of the Mesopotamian city of Ur is named Abram. One day, when he is seventy-five years old, Abram receives a call from God to leave his home and go to a land God will show him. This is certainly an unprecedented and curious occurrence, yet we are told, "So Abram left" (Genesis 12:4).

He travels with his wife, Sarai, his nephew Lot, his household, his servants, and his flocks. Abra(ha)m continues to be one of the Bible's preeminent examples of faith, yet he is not without his faults. Twice when he feels threatened by foreign powers, he passes off his wife as his sister, allowing her to be added to other men's harems. But both times God protects her and returns her, honor intact, to Abram (Genesis 12:10–20, 20:1–17).

Still, Abram is no coward. When Lot is kidnapped by a coalition of kings, Abram leads a rescue party to get him back. And when a major disagreement breaks out between the servants of Abram and the servants of Lot, it is Uncle Abe who settles the matter by giving Lot his choice of land on which to settle. (Lot unwisely chooses the cities of Sodom and Gomorrah.)

As Abram continues to act in faith, God continues to add to what he has promised him. God promised to make Abram's name great, to create from him a great nation, to give him all the land he could see in every direction, and to give him descendants as numerous as the stars in the sky. And as one sign of his covenant with Abram, God changes Abram's name to Abraham: "father of many."

The problem is that Abraham doesn't yet have a child, and he and Sarah (whose name is also changed by God) are aging fast. So when Abraham reaches eighty-six (and Sarah is only ten years younger), Sarah has him sleep with her servant, Hagar, in order to produce an offspring. The resulting child, Ishmael, creates friction within the household. God also reaffirms that Abraham's child is to come from Sarah.

And sure enough, when Abraham is a hundred and Sarah is ninety, she gives birth to their son and names him Isaac. Through Isaac the Jewish nation will come to be . . . and through Ishmael, the Arab people. Abram, whose original name meant "exalted father," does indeed become Abraham, the "father of many," and is now revered by the Christians, Jews, and Muslims.

Sodom and Gomorrah (GENESIS 18–19)

Abraham's nephew Lot has settled in the twin cities of sin: Sodom and Gomorrah. God tells Abraham he is planning to destroy the cities. Abraham barters with God, finally getting God to agree to spare the cities if there are even ten righteous people living there. But there aren't.

When a couple of angels go to warn Lot that God is about to destroy his city, a gang of local men attempt to break into Lot's house and have sex with them (thinking they are merely male visitors). The angels strike the crowd with blindness and tell Lot to have his friends and family leave immediately. But when Lot does so, they think he is joking.

At dawn the angels physically pull Lot, his wife, and their two daughters out of the city to safety, telling them to flee to the mountains and warning them not to look back. But Lot's wife turns to look and instantly becomes a pillar of salt. Not long afterward, Lot's daughters take turns getting him drunk and sleeping with him so they can bear children. From their sons, Moab and Ben-Ammi, arise the Moabites and Ammonites, tribes that will cause the Israelites much trouble throughout their history.

Isaac (GENESIS 21–22, 24, 26)

Perhaps the best-known story of Abraham involves his son Isaac. When Isaac is still young, God tests Abraham, instructing him to offer his son as a sacrifice. Abraham responds "early the next morning." The two go to the top of a mountain where Abraham ties down Isaac, raises a knife, and prepares to plunge it into his son. At the last second, an angel calls out to stop him. A ram caught in the underbrush serves as a sacrifice instead, and Abraham passes his test of faith. In the New Testament we are told that Abraham believed

God could raise Isaac from the dead if that's what it took for God to keep his promise (Hebrews 11:17–19).

Later another great Bible story tells of how Abraham sends a servant to find a godly wife for Isaac. In what is clearly an act of God, the servant brings back Rebekah. In a case of "like father, like son," when Isaac finds himself confronted with a foreign king who is attracted to his wife, he says she is his sister and allows her to go with the king. But when the king happens to look out a window and see Isaac and Rebekah making out, it doesn't take him long to figure out that something is wrong. The situation is resolved peacefully, and eventually Isaac and Rebekah become the parents of twins: Jacob and Esau.

Jacob (GENESIS 25:19–34, 27–33)

To be twins, you couldn't find two more opposite people than Jacob and Esau. Jacob is described as "a quiet man, staying among the tents." Esau is the pride of his father and "a skillful hunter, a man of the open country" (Genesis 25:27).

As the older son, Esau should have the "birthright"—all the blessing and benefits usually granted the oldest male in the family. But depending on how you read the Bible, Jacob is either a selfish and wily con man or a masterful and shrewd businessman. (Even as they came out of the womb, Jacob's hand was grasping Esau's heel.) Jacob first catches Esau at a vulnerable moment and gets him to agree to give up his birthright. And later, when Isaac is about to bestow the formal blessing on his older son, Jacob and Rebekah put together an elaborate scheme that completely deceives the twins' blind father, leaving Jacob with the blessing. As a result, he has to leave home to escape Esau's rage.

In his twenty years away, Jacob has a prophetic dream of a staircase into heaven, takes two wives, has eleven sons and a daughter, and accumulates great herds of animals while working for Rebekah's brother, Laban. As he is preparing to return home and confront Esau, he spends a night wrestling with a stranger who turns out to be God. At that point, God changes Jacob's name to Israel (meaning "he struggles with God"). And Jacob's sons become, essentially, the twelve tribes of Israel, or collectively, the Israelites.

After twenty years, Esau has forgiven Jacob and the two reconcile peacefully.

Joseph (GENESIS 37, 39–50)

Of all his sons, Jacob's favorite by far is Joseph—for many years the only child of Rachel, his true love. A rivalry develops between Joseph and his ten older brothers that becomes so bad that they decide to kill him. But when a caravan comes through, they opt to sell Joseph into slavery instead. To cover their act, they take the fancy coat their father had given Joseph, dip it in goat's blood, and tell Jacob that a wild animal has killed Joseph.

Joseph matures quickly after he is taken to Egypt. He is a faithful servant, both to God and his master, Potiphar, yet Potiphar's wife falsely accuses him of attempted rape and gets him thrown into prison. Even in jail, Joseph's continued faithfulness is rewarded, as he is quickly promoted to oversee the other inmates, leaving the warden with nothing to worry about.

On his eventual release, Joseph interprets a dream for Pharaoh and foresees a seven-year abundant harvest followed by a seven-year drought and famine. Thanks to Joseph, Egypt stocks up on grain, is prepared during the years of famine, and even has enough food stored to supply the surrounding countries. In addition, Joseph is promoted to second in command over the country, subject only to Pharaoh himself.

As an added twist, when the famine hits Israel, Jacob sends his sons to Egypt to buy grain. And there, standing before Joseph and begging for food, are his ten brothers. They don't recognize him, but he knows *them*. He creates a number of situations to see if they have changed, and indeed, they are feeling remorse for their past actions and are emphatically protective of their new "little brother," Benjamin. Eventually, Joseph reveals his identity and extends his forgiveness, assuring them that it was God's plan all along.

Jacob, of course, is overjoyed to discover that Joseph is still alive. And the Egyptian Pharaoh even insists that Joseph's family move to Egypt and live in "the best part of the land"—the region of Goshen (Genesis 47:6).

The book of Genesis concludes with the deaths of Jacob (Israel) and Joseph. But before his death, Joseph makes his brothers swear an oath that when they leave Egypt they will carry his bones with them. It seems a strange request, but as we're about to see, maybe Joseph knew something they didn't.

THREE

The Wilderness

Out of Egypt and Home Again

As our journey through the Bible continues, we will stay in Egypt and let about four hundred years pass. During that time, the Israelite presence continues to grow. The seventy people from Joseph's family who migrated to Goshen become a formidable force of hundreds of thousands. Meanwhile, the Egyptian leaders forget about Joseph and his God-given wisdom that allowed Egypt to prosper during a horrible widespread famine.

Moses: His Birth, His Felony, and the Burning Bush (EXODUS 1–3)

As a result, the new Pharaoh has decided to enslave the Israelites. And to make things worse, a command has gone out to kill all male Hebrew babies by throwing them into the Nile River. It is under this death sentence that Moses is born.

But rather than obey the edict, Moses' mother coats a basket with pitch, places it among the reeds of the Nile, and has his big sister watch to see what will happen. The baby cries just as Pharaoh's daughter is taking her bath, and she adopts him, even hiring his own mother to be his wet nurse.

Moses grows up Egyptian, but he is aware of his Hebrew roots. One day, upon witnessing an Egyptian beating a Hebrew, he kills the Egyptian while no one is looking—or so he thinks. But when he discovers that people know what he has done, he flees into the wilderness to escape Pharaoh's wrath. There he marries Zipporah, one of seven daughters of a man named Jethro, and works as a shepherd for his father-in-law.

While out with the sheep one day, Moses comes upon a bush that appears to be burning yet does not burn up. God addresses him by name from the bush and tells him to go lead his people out of Egypt "into a good and spacious land, a land flowing with milk and honey" (Exodus 3:8). Moses is reluctant and offers a number of excuses, but he eventually obeys.

Pharaoh, the Plagues, the Exodus, and the Red Sea (EXODUS 4–14)

Moses returns to Pharaoh and tells him to "let my people go," just as God has instructed, but Pharaoh only intensifies the workload of the Israelites. God then sends a series of plagues upon Egypt—frogs, locusts, hail, darkness, and more. Pharaoh resists plague after plague, even though his country is in turmoil while the land where the Israelites live is spared. But in a final plague, God strikes down the firstborn in all human and livestock families. The Israelites have prepared ahead of time by placing lamb's blood on their doorposts, causing God to pass over their houses with no harm (and instituting the Jewish celebration of Passover). But the deaths in the Egyptian homes are finally what convince Pharaoh to relent and let the Israelites leave.

However, Moses and his people don't get far when Pharaoh changes his mind. The Israelites are camped at the Red Sea as the Egyptian army rides up. The Israelites seem to be trapped, but God instructs Moses to hold his staff over the water, and as he does, the waters part. The Israelites cross on dry ground. As the Egyptians try to follow, their chariot wheels come off and they realize that "the LORD is fighting . . . against Egypt!" (Exodus 14:25). But too late. The waters come down and there are no Egyptian survivors.

Forty Years in the Wilderness

(EXODUS 15–40, LEVITICUS, NUMBERS, DEUTERONOMY)

The presence of God goes before the people in a pillar of cloud by day and a pillar of fire by night. He leads them in a somewhat circuitous route to prevent encounters with threatening nations. He provides fresh water, even from polluted pools and solid rock. He causes manna, which tastes "like wafers made with honey," to fall every day (except the Sabbaths) (Exodus 16:31).

Along the way, God has the people stop at Sinai, where he calls Moses to the top of the mountain and gives him laws for the people to live by, including the Ten Commandments (see page 98). God also provides specific plans for the construction of a tabernacle, a portable house of worship for the people during their travels (and precursor to the temple).

But in spite of everything God is doing for them, the people perpetually complain. They don't like the monotony of manna. They fear they will run out of food and water, and that enemies will overpower them. They keep wanting—sometimes demanding—to return to Egypt where at least they knew what was in store for them (although that meant slavery)!

Even at the edge of the promised land, their final destination, they balk. Twelve spies are sent to scout out the land. It is truly a wonderful place, but the natives are large and intimidating. Ten of the spies recommend turning around and going back. Only two—Joshua and Caleb—insist on entering, and those two are almost stoned by the crowd.

But God has had enough. He is ready to strike the people down with a plague and start over, but Moses intercedes. So instead, God decrees that they must wander in the wilderness for forty years until the unbelieving generation has died off and is replaced by more faithful people. Upon hearing the news, the remorseful Israelites *then* try to enter the land and are severely routed (Numbers 13–14).

And sure enough, forty years later the new generation of Israelites is ready to move forward. Moses has been forbidden to enter the promised land because of a frustration-inspired act of disobedience, but God takes him onto a mountain and allows him to see the land before he dies. So it is Joshua who eventually takes the people into the land.

Here are a few important stories from this section of the Bible:

- The bones of Joseph travel with the Israelites (Exodus 13:17–19)
- The golden calf (Exodus 32)
- Moses' sin (Numbers 20:1–13; Deuteronomy 34)
- Balaam and his talking donkey (Numbers 22)
- The Ten Commandments (Exodus 20:3–17; Deuteronomy 5:7–21)
- Rahab and the Israelite spies (Joshua 2)
- A miraculous entry into the promised land (Joshua 3)

- Achan: The effects of one person's sin on a nation (Joshua 7)

Joshua and the Promised Land (BOOK OF JOSHUA)

Joshua is an exemplary leader, personally chosen by God to complete the Israelites' journey. The mighty city of Jericho is the first obstacle they face in the new land, but Joshua follows God's instructions to the letter and the walls come tumbling down.

After establishing themselves in the promised land, the Israelites divide into tribes and go to their respective areas that God has assigned to them. Their assignment is to completely clear out the natives of the area and establish themselves. They are to show no mercy and to have no interaction with the non-Israelite peoples.

The people are strong and God is with them, yet very few of the tribes do as they have been instructed. If they rid the new land of potential oppressors, they could live in peace and prosperity for a long while. But they don't. And in the next chapter we'll see what happens as a result.

FOUR

Settling Down

Building a Nation

So far in our rapid journey through the Bible, the action has moved from Mesopotamia to Israel, to Egypt, and back to Israel again (the promised land). It is here that the action will take place for a while. Sadly, the people will eventually be forced to leave, but for the next few centuries they will be settling in.

The Judges

The "judges" of this biblical era are by no means what we imagine when we think of courtrooms, flowing robes, and rules of order. The biblical judges are warrior leaders of the nation, called by God to confront powerful enemies during a rough and barbaric time. After the people have settled in the promised land, it doesn't take long for the spiritual commitment of

Israel to decline and then disappear altogether. The motto of this era is well described in the final verse of the book of Judges: "In those days Israel had no king; everyone did as he saw fit" (Judges 21:25).

The book of Judges describes a repeated cycle: (1) people forget about God, (2) God allows various enemies to conquer and rule the Israelites, (3) the Israelites repent and cry out to God for help, (4) God calls a judge to confront and defeat Israel's enemies, (5) the nation has a lengthy time of peace and freedom. And each time, the people again forget about God, starting yet another cycle.

Of the thirteen or so judges who rule, the better known ones are Deborah, Gideon, and Samson.

Deborah (JUDGES 4–5)

The judge of this era should be a man named Barak, but he is a hesitant leader. Deborah is a prophetess who tells Barak what he should do, but his reluctance to respond results in Deborah's taking the lead. In addition to Deborah and her leadership, another woman helps end Israel's oppression. Although Deborah and Barak have already routed the enemy, the opposing leader has escaped and is hiding in the tent of a friend. But the wife of that friend, a woman named Jael, puts the evil leader to sleep and then drives a tent peg through his head.

Gideon (JUDGES 6–8)

Gideon is definitely not the world's most dynamic leader. When we first see him, he is threshing wheat in a winepress to avoid being seen by the vicious Midianites, who would most certainly help themselves to his grain. Nevertheless, an angel suddenly appears and says: "The LORD is with you, mighty warrior" (Judges 6:12).

Gideon does everything God asks of him, even when he doesn't seem to have a lot of confidence in himself. He is the one who asks for a sign from God by placing a wool fleece on the ground and asking that in the morning the fleece be wet with dew while the ground be completely dry. And when God does as Gideon asks, Gideon asks for the reverse to occur. The next morning the ground is covered with dew, but the fleece is dry.

God wants to show Gideon what he, God, can do. Gideon has an army of thirty-two thousand soldiers, but God tells him to send home everyone who is scared. Immediately, twenty-two thousand men leave. Then God reduces the remaining ten thousand to only three hundred. And even then, by following God's instructions, the three hundred Israelites defeat the entire Midianite army using torches, pitchers, and trumpets rather than swords. A God-initiated panic causes the Midianites to turn on one another and flee. Thanks to Gideon, the Israelites experience peace for forty years.

Samson (JUDGES 13–16)

Samson is Gideon's opposite. At God's instructions, Samson's parents raise him as a Nazirite, which means in part that he will never drink wine, eat grape products, or get a haircut (Numbers 6:1–21). Other biblical Nazirites were Samuel (1 Samuel 1:11) and John the Baptist (Luke 1:15).

God has given Samson extraordinary strength, which Samson takes for granted. He disregards his parents' wishes, goes where he wants, gets into fights, and is a sore loser when outsmarted. Even so, God uses Samson to retaliate against the Philistines, who are oppressing Israel at the time. Samson sleeps with their women, single-handedly kills a thousand of their men in a skirmish, removes and carries away their city gates, and escapes every time they try to trap him.

So the Philistines use Samson's self-interest against him. Samson falls in love with a Philistine woman named Delilah, whom the other Philistines hire to find the secret of his strength. He holds out for a while, but eventually he lets her know that his strength is connected to his long hair. When he awakes from a nap, he discovers he is bound and has had a haircut. For the first time in his life, he is helpless.

The Philistines blind Samson and force him to work for them. But when his hair grows back out, his strength returns. At a large religious gathering where the Philistines are making fun of Samson, he pulls down the central pillars of their temple, killing thousands of Philistines and dying in the process.

King Saul (1 SAMUEL 8–31)

After the era of the judges, a prophet-judge named Samuel becomes God's choice of leader. But by this time, the people are demanding a king because "then we will be like all the other nations" (1 Samuel 8:20). The Law that was handed down from Moses has provided for a human king (Deuteronomy 17:14–20), although God is supposed to be Israel's king. But God tells Samuel to do as the people have asked.

The first king is Saul, described as "an impressive young man without equal among the Israelites—a head taller than any of the others" (1 Samuel 9:2). The Philistines are still around and are a constant threat to Israel. Saul has some early military victories, and so does his courageous son, Jonathan. But Saul's faith seems to wane in his later years, and he isn't as obedient as he should be. So God begins to prepare another king "after his own heart" (1 Samuel 13:14) to replace Saul.

Saul even consults a witch (medium) for advice, and soon afterward he kills himself after being wounded in a lost battle.

David (1 SAMUEL 16–2 SAMUEL 24)

David is God's choice to replace Saul, but the switch isn't quick or easy. First David makes a name for himself by killing the giant Goliath and then winning a number of battles against the Philistines. Saul's jealously intensifies to the point where he repeatedly tries to kill David. But David refuses to fight back, even though he twice has an ideal opportunity to kill Saul.

After Saul's death, David unites the tribes of Israel and establishes Jerusalem as the capital of the combined kingdom. David seems to do everything right, until later in life when he sees Bathsheba taking a bath, sends for her, and sleeps with her. When she conceives a child while her husband is away at battle, David arranges to have her husband killed. God sends a prophet to confront David, and the child of the affair dies.

In addition, David's life is never again the same. One of his sons (Amnon) rapes his half-sister, and another son (Absalom) kills Amnon. In time, Absalom even tries to take over the kingdom from David and dies as a result.

But David repents of his sin. Many of the Psalms are attributed to him, and Psalm 51 is a stark and humble confession of his affair with Bathsheba. Later, David and Bathsheba have another son, Solomon, who will become the next king.

Solomon (1 KINGS 1–11)

David has united the kingdom and conquered Israel's enemies. Solomon begins his reign with peace and quickly establishes a period of prosperity unlike any other in Israel's history. Early on, God offers to give Solomon anything he asks for. Because Solomon asks for wisdom to lead his people, rather than for riches or honor, God gives him wisdom *and* riches *and* honor.

Solomon's great wisdom quickly becomes evident in everything from lawsuits between prostitutes vying for child custody to visits from the queen of Sheba. He writes thousands of proverbs and songs. People come from all over the world just to listen to him. And the wealth of Israel reaches the point where "the king made silver as common in Jerusalem as stones" (1 Kings 10:27). Under Solomon's rule the boundaries of Israel extend farther than ever before, or since.

Solomon's most significant accomplishment is the building of the temple in Jerusalem. It is a magnificent building dedicated to God. Following the design of the tabernacle, it has a Holy Place, where only priests can enter, and a Most Holy Place where only the high priest can go, and then only once a year, on the Day of Atonement, in order to offer a sacrifice for the sins of the nation.

But in later life Solomon turns to idolatry. He has married seven hundred wives and also has three hundred concubines. Because of his devotion to his wives and their gods, "his heart was not fully devoted to the LORD his God, as the heart of David his father had been" (1 Kings 11:4). As a result, God decrees that the kingdom will soon be divided. Israel is never again the same. It is a sad finish to a remarkable life.

Other good stories from this part of the Bible include:

- Ruth, Naomi, and Boaz provide a poignant love story during the time of the judges (the book of Ruth)
- Samuel receives a call from God (1 Samuel 3)
- David defeats Goliath (1 Samuel 17)
- The strong bonds of friendship between David and Saul's son Jonathan (1 Samuel 20)
- David spares Saul's life—twice! (1 Samuel 24, 26)
- Saul visits a medium at Endor (1 Samuel 28)
- The death of Absalom (2 Samuel 18)
- Solomon suggests cutting a baby in half (1 Kings 3:16–28)
- The queen of Sheba visits Solomon (1 Kings 10:1–13)

We will pick up the action of the Bible from this point in chapter 6. But first, let's look at some classic literature of the time.

FIVE

Wisdom Literature

Songs, Stories, Sayings, and Sex

We have been following the action of the Bible from Creation to the unification of the twelve tribes into a prosperous nation. Now we're going to pause to quickly examine some of the exquisite writings of the Bible.

The Book of Job

The story of Job is a distinctive book among the other sixty-five in the Bible. While the other Wisdom books are songs, sayings, and expressions of an author, the book of Job is a narrative of a man who appears to have lived during the times of the patriarchs.

Job is exemplary in his righteousness—so much so that God notes, "There is no one on earth like him." But Satan challenges God's claim, saying that since

God has blessed Job with so much, *of course* he has no trouble living a "blameless and upright" life (Job 1:8). Satan asks to take away everything Job has.

So one day a series of messengers arrives at Job's home, each with tragic news. Sabeans have carried off all his oxen and donkeys. A fire has burned up the sheep and his servants. Chaldean raiding parties have taken all his camels. And even worse, Job's ten children have all died in a sudden desert storm.

Job, of course, is devastated, yet he "did not sin by charging God with wrongdoing" (Job 1:22). When God points this out, Satan scoffs and says that if Job's health is affected, then he will crack. So Job is afflicted with painful sores over his entire body. He sits among the ashes and scrapes himself with pieces of broken pottery. His wife is no help. Her advice: "Curse God and die!" But Job has a different outlook: "Shall we accept good from God, and not trouble?" (Job 2:9–10).

All this happens in the first two chapters of the book of Job. Then, for the next thirty-five chapters, Job is visited by four friends and they discuss why he is suffering. They insist that he must have done something wrong, which he persistently denies. Yet he can't understand (much less explain) his dire circumstances.

Finally, God appears, and he and Job dialogue. (More accurately, God talks and Job listens.) Through a lengthy series of questions, God demonstrates that there is much that Job doesn't understand about life on earth. Job realizes that God is in charge, and he is content with that knowledge. And God gives Job "twice as much as he had before" and another family (Job 42:10). Job dies at age 140, "old and full of years" (Job 42:17).

The Book of Psalms

The book of Psalms is a collection of songs from a number of sources and are used for various purposes. The 150 psalms make up the longest book in the Bible. About half of them are attributed to David, two to Solomon, one to Moses, and several to various other writers. Forty-nine of them remain anonymous.

An emphasis of the Psalms is praise to God. Some are personal and confessional. Others are appropriate for public and group use, including Psalms 120–134. It is thought that these "songs of ascent" were used in temple worship and perhaps by travelers making a pilgrimage "up" to Jerusalem.

The most familiar psalm is probably Psalm 23 (see page 99). The longest one is Psalm 119, at 176 verses. The shortest is Psalm 117, at only 2 verses. Psalm 22 was quoted in part by Jesus on the cross and is one of seventeen specifically messianic psalms.

Whether expressing thanksgiving, sorrow, frustration, or joy, the Psalms are very open and honest expressions to God. Many are surprisingly bold in their frankness.

The Book of Proverbs

One of the key themes of Proverbs is wisdom, so it is no surprise that Solomon is believed to be a major contributor, yet other wise people contributed as well.

Parts of the book are essay-like writings about various topics: exhortations to embrace wisdom (Proverbs 1:8–4:27); admonitions against adultery and folly (Proverbs 5–7); qualities of "a wife of noble character" (Proverbs 31:10–31); and so on. Other portions contain long lists of not necessarily related wise sayings.

Some of our common sayings find their roots in Proverbs. For example:

- He who spares the rod hates his son, but he who loves him is careful to discipline him.
  (Proverbs 13:24)
- A gentle answer turns away wrath, but a harsh word stirs up anger. (Proverbs 15:1)
- Pride goes before destruction, a haughty spirit before a fall. (Proverbs 16:18)
- Train a child in the way he should go, and when he is old he will not turn from it. (Proverbs 22:6)

Other proverbs are more obscure, yet no less pointed:

- Like a gold ring in a pig's snout is a beautiful woman who shows no discretion. (Proverbs 11:22)
- Better to live on a corner of the roof than share a house with a quarrelsome wife. (Proverbs 21:9). (And with seven hundred wives, Solomon should know!)
- If a man loudly blesses his neighbor early in the morning, it will be taken as a curse. (Proverbs 27:14)

Proverbs is a good book to skim through when time permits. You're likely to be a bit wiser once you do.

The Book of Ecclesiastes

"'Meaningless! Meaningless!' says the Teacher. 'Utterly meaningless! Everything is meaningless'" (Ecclesiastes 1:1).

And with that jolly opening, the book of Ecclesiastes begins. Many believe the Teacher to be Solomon. If not, it was someone in a similar position of wealth, power, and opportunity.

The writer leads a determined search for meaning in life. He seeks meaning in pleasure: "I denied myself nothing my eyes desired" (Ecclesiastes 2:10). Yet he finds no satisfaction. He tries working hard, only to realize he will die and leave everything to someone else who hasn't worked for it (Ecclesiastes 2:21). He tries a number of pursuits, only to find them to be "meaningless, a chasing after the wind" (Ecclesiastes 2:26).

Eventually, he decides that the best anyone can do is "to eat and drink, and to find satisfaction in his toilsome labor" (Ecclesiastes 5:18). And his final conclusion? "Fear God and keep his commandments, for this is the whole duty of man" (Ecclesiastes 12:13). Acknowledgment of God's presence and involvement can add meaning to life when nothing else does.

The Song of Songs

From the frequently bleak and perplexing book of Ecclesiastes we come to the Song of Songs, which provides an altogether different experience. This writing, also attributed to Solomon, is a bold and sometimes explicit love story. It is structured as a dialogue between the Beloved (the girl) and the Lover (the guy), with occasional commentary from friends.

Among the more graphic passages is the Lover's comment: "Your stature is like that of the palm, and your breasts like clusters of fruit. I said, 'I will climb the palm tree; I will take hold of its fruit'" (Song of Songs 7:7–8). (Some Bible passages don't need much expert interpretation.)

But more true to the book as a whole is one of its closing comments:

> Love is as strong as death,
>> its jealousy unyielding as the grave.
> It burns like blazing fire,
>> like a mighty flame.
> Many waters cannot quench love;
>> rivers cannot wash it away.
> If one were to give
>> all the wealth of his house for love,
> it would be utterly scorned. (SONG OF SONGS 8:6–7)

Some people interpret the Song of Songs to be symbolic of the relationship between God and his people (whether Israel or the church). Perhaps it is. But it also stands alone as a lasting and classic song of love, wisdom, and romance.

A few short summaries can't do justice to the beautiful poetry and sentiment expressed in these biblical writings. But since this is a *Bible to Go*, we must return to the action of the Old Testament ... bleak though it is.

Divided and Conquered

The Fall of the Nation
and the Rise of the Prophets

Well, we've hit the high point of the Old Testament, and it's pretty much downhill from here. Now we begin a long, extended spiritual slide with tragic (though not unforeseen) results.

A Kingdom Divided Against Itself

(1 KINGS 12–2 KINGS 25)

After Solomon sets aside all his wisdom to forsake God in favor of his many wives, it doesn't take long for the kingdom to begin to crumble. One of Solomon's officers, Jeroboam, rebels and soon becomes king of the ten-plus tribes that make up the northern kingdom (Israel). But because of David's previous faithfulness, God ensures that a portion of the nation remains in the family. Solomon's son Rehoboam becomes king of the tribe of Judah and a portion of the territory of Benjamin (known collectively as Judah). From this point on, the kingdom is divided, with each part having a succession of about twenty kings over the next 200 to 350 years.

After Saul, David, and Solomon, the kings of Israel and Judah are for the most part ineffective and inconsequential. All that is recorded for many of them is: "He did evil in the eyes of the LORD." In fact, as soon as the kingdom splits and Jeroboam sees the allure of the temple in Judah, he sets up a couple of golden calves in the northern kingdom to keep the people from feeling the need to go to Jerusalem to offer sacrifices. The God-given Mosaic Law is quickly forgotten.

And Judah does little better than Israel at maintaining a shred of spiritual integrity. Both kingdoms grow weak and vulnerable. The northern tribes are conquered and exiled to Assyria in 722 BC. The people of Judah hold out almost another century and a half before falling and being carted off to Babylon in 586 BC. But the sieges are awful, with priests slaughtered and starving mothers reduced to cannibalism of their own children (Lamentations 2:20, 4:9–10).

Ahab and Jezebel
(1 KINGS 16:29–22:40; 2 KINGS 9:30–37)

Sadly, it is the evil kings who are remembered more than the decent ones from this period of biblical history. Not too many people recall Jehoshaphat (1 Kings 22:41–50), Jotham (2 Kings 15:32–38), Hezekiah (2 Kings 18–20), or Josiah (2 Kings 22:1–23:30), who went against the tide of the time and were relatively righteous and faithful.

Instead, we hear more about Ahab and Jezebel: "There was never a man like Ahab, who sold himself to do evil in the eyes of the LORD, urged on by Jezebel his wife" (1 Kings 21:25). They worship Baal and Asherah rather than God. They make life very difficult for the prophet Elijah. And when a simple man named Naboth refuses to sell them a vineyard they want, they frame him and have him stoned to death for a false charge.

Elijah prophesied that for murdering an innocent man, both Ahab and Jezebel will be devoured by dogs, and his prophecies come to pass.

Elijah and Elisha (1 KINGS 17–2 KINGS 13:21)

When the kings of Israel and Judah stop providing spiritual leadership for the nations, God sends prophets to proclaim his truth to the people. Elijah and Elisha are bright spots in the spiritual darkness of the series of evil kings. Not only does God provide for them in unusual ways—such as being fed by ravens (1 Kings 17:1–6)—but they also receive power to perform all kinds of miracles: making lost ax heads float, calling fire from heaven, healing leprosy, and even bringing back people from the dead. At the end of his years of faithful service, Elijah is taken to heaven in a chariot of fire (2 Kings 2:1–18).

Numerous prophets are mentioned by name in the Bible, Elijah and Elisha being two of the more prominent ones. Others wrote books to record the events and messages of their ministries. The writers of the longer books are known as the Major Prophets (Isaiah, Jeremiah, Ezekiel, and Daniel). Those with shorter writings are called Minor Prophets.

Isaiah

Isaiah describes a magnificent vision he has when God first calls him to be a prophet (Isaiah 6). His outlook on the future includes both short-term events (the fall of Israel to the Assyrians and the eventual fall of Judah to the Babylonians) and long-range prophecies about the coming Messiah. Some of his more popular messianic predictions are found in Isaiah 7:14, 9:2–7, 11:1–9, and 53:1–12. His writings are frequently quoted in the New Testament.

Jeremiah

Jeremiah is sometimes called "the weeping prophet." His message of coming judgment is not a popular one. At least once his scroll of prophecies is burned (Jeremiah 36). At times people threaten his life if he doesn't quit prophesying (Jeremiah 11:18–23); another time he is tossed into a pit and left to die, but a friend helps him escape (Jeremiah 38:1–13).

And if Jeremiah's life weren't sad enough, his name comes up most often as the author of the book of Lamentations, a series of five laments detailing the fall of Jerusalem. Yet Jeremiah remains faithful and weathers the many storms of his long and dedicated life.

Ezekiel

Like Isaiah, Ezekiel has an amazing vision of God in his heaven and an unmistakable call to serve as a prophet (Ezekiel 1–2). He is among the captives carried off to Babylon, and he ministers to his people there. One of the most remarkable of Ezekiel's many visions is of a valley filled with dry bones. But when God's breath enters the bones, they are once again covered with tendons, flesh, and skin. The vision is a promise that God will restore his people and return them to Israel—no matter how hopeless their situation looks at the time (Ezekiel 37:1–14).

Daniel

Daniel is also taken into captivity. He has a God-given ability to interpret dreams, which keeps him in favor with a series of kings: Nebuchadnezzar and Belshazzar of Babylon, and Darius the Mede. Most people know about his lions' den incident (Daniel 6), which occurs late in his life. He also interprets Nebuchadnezzar's dream of an enormous statue felled by a "rock cut out of a mountain, but not by human hands" (Daniel 2:45)—a foretelling of the coming of Jesus. He later interprets mysterious writing on the wall (Daniel 5). In Daniel's book we also read the story of his friends Shadrach, Meshach, and Abednego, and their ordeal in the fiery furnace (Daniel 3). And the last half of the book (Daniel 7–12) contains prophecies that many people use to help interpret Revelation and explain the expected events of the end times.

The Minor Prophets

The Minor Prophets are Hosea, Joel, Amos, Obadiah, Jonah, Micah, Nahum, Habakkuk, Zephaniah, Haggai, Zechariah, and Malachi. Of these dozen men, the best known is Jonah because of his fascinating story of surviving three days in the belly of a great fish. Hosea's life is also interesting because he marries an adulterous woman who later leaves him and has kids with other men. Still, he takes her back to demonstrate God's persistent faithfulness to his people. Micah tells us where to look for the Messiah to be born (Micah 5:2).

And the other Minor Prophets have valuable insights into both their own times and the times to come.

The writings of the prophets are probably some of the least-read in the Bible. Yet their contribution to both their people and the totality of the Bible should never be underestimated. Though largely unknown to today's population, they all provide testimony to God's grace and mercy . . . even in the worst of times.

SEVEN

Back Home

The Return to Jerusalem

The Bible doesn't say a lot about the people who were taken to Assyria after their exile, although the spiritual reasons for their deportation are clearly listed (2 Kings 17). We read that the leader of Assyria carried them away and replaced them with people from Arab countries. But considerably more is said of the people from Judah who were taken to Babylon.

If you happen to be following along in a Bible as you read this book, you will notice that a couple of chapters back, we skipped over a few Bible books. The books of 1 and 2 Chronicles were not referenced because they contain much of the same content as the books of Samuel and Kings. But we saved the books of Ezra, Nehemiah, and Esther for this point. Chronologically, the events of those books took place during and after the people of Judah went into captivity—some of the final events of the Old Testament.

Esther

Ladies first: let's look at Esther. Her story takes place during the exile, and the other stories occur slightly later.

The Babylonians have conquered Judah, but not long afterward, the Medes and Persians then defeat the Babylonians. A ruler named Xerxes comes to power. His wife defies him one day, so he banishes her and begins a search for a new queen.

Esther has a relative named Mordecai who advises her to attempt to become queen. She does, and she is chosen above all the other hopeful contenders. But Xerxes doesn't know she is a Jew.

As it turns out, one of Xerxes' top officials, Haman, is plotting to annihilate the Jews. Esther learns of the plot and, at risk of her life, approaches the king to ask if she can schedule a dinner party for Haman. Xerxes is glad to grant her request. Later, on the very night that Haman is planning to get the king's permission to eliminate all Jews, Esther reveals her ethnicity and tells Xerxes: "I and my people have been sold for destruction and slaughter and annihilation" (Esther 7:4). Xerxes is furious, and Haman is hanged that night.

The Jewish feast of Purim commemorates this event. Although the name of God is never mentioned in the book of Esther, the many "coincidental" events and ironies of the story reflect his presence and protection.

Ezra

The prophet Jeremiah had foretold that the Israelites' captivity in Babylon would last only seventy years (Jeremiah 25:11–12, 29:10–14). After Persia defeats Babylon, the Persian king, Cyrus, is inclined to let the Jewish captives return to their homeland. In fact, Cyrus allows everyone to leave who wants to and even returns many of the furnishings that had been taken from their temple.

The problem is that the temple has been destroyed. So one of the first tasks of the returning Israelites is to rebuild it. Among the first groups to return to Israel is a man named Zerubbabel, who has been appointed governor. His group faces considerable opposition from the people who have settled in the area, yet they persevere and rebuild the temple. Ezra is a priest who comes with a subsequent group of exiles to help attend to the task. A joyful dedication and celebration follow the completion of the rebuilt temple (Ezra 6:16–22).

But it was brought to Ezra's attention that many of the men, including certain priests, have intermarried

BUSINESS REPLY MAIL
FIRST-CLASS MAIL PERMIT NO 220 RED OAK IA

POSTAGE WILL BE PAID BY ADDRESSEE

Popular Mechanics

PO BOX 7168
RED OAK IA 51591-2168

with nonbelieving women. Ezra calls for a period of confession and repentance, which is followed by the discovery that over one hundred people have married foreign wives. These men agree to divorce their nonbelieving wives and send them away, along with their children.

Nehemiah

Nehemiah returns to his homeland in yet another caravan. His group sets out to rebuild the walls around Jerusalem. They, too, face a number of troublemakers who try to thwart their efforts, going so far as to make attempts on Nehemiah's life. Nehemiah is both faithful and practical, so "we prayed to our God and posted a guard day and night to meet this threat" (Nehemiah 4:9).

After the city walls are completed, Ezra assembles the people and reads from the Mosaic Law as "all the people listened attentively" (Nehemiah 8:3). The people weep as they realize how they have disregarded God's law for so long. But Ezra and Nehemiah tell them to eat and rejoice because the event is a celebration. So they feast and worship for more than a week. It is the biggest celebration they have held since the days of Joshua, "and their joy was very great" (Nehemiah 8:17–18).

Between the Testaments

As the Old Testament closes, the Hebrew people are allowed to return to their homeland, though they are still under Persian rule. About four centuries pass between the close of the Old Testament and the start of the New Testament. During that time, the Greeks defeat the Persians just as the Persians had conquered the Babylonians. However, the Greeks want to hellenize the world: unify all territories under Greek language and Greek customs.

One particularly headstrong leader named Antiochus IV Epiphanes takes a personal interest in seeing that all Jewish writings and customs are destroyed. But he pushes too hard. One Jewish family rises up in defiance, and others follow. The elder of the family is named Mattathias and has five sons. The oldest, Judas (Maccabeus), gave name to the Maccabean revolt that lasted from 166 BC to 142 BC. The Jewish people are victorious and earn their independence.

But soon the Roman Empire comes to power. After a lengthy siege, in 63 BC the Romans take over Jerusalem, slaughter priests, and defile the Most Holy Place in the temple. So, as the New Testament begins, many of the Jewish people still feel a lot of animosity toward Rome. Keep that in mind as we continue our journey through the Bible.

Jesus

His Humanity

Throughout the Old Testament . . . especially during bad times . . . the people were told to expect a Messiah. For centuries, God's people had been watching and waiting for a Savior. Now, with the oppression they are feeling from Rome, no doubt some of them recall the many promises that God would send someone to help.

In the flow of Bible history, everything points to the life, death, and resurrection of Jesus. Many previous events and prophecies have foreshadowed this, and everything afterward will point back to the significance of Jesus, the Messiah, the Christ ("anointed one").

Jesus' Birth (MATTHEW 1–2; LUKE 1–2)

The first we see of Jesus in the Bible, he doesn't look much like the Savior of the world. God chooses to send him to earth as a baby, to live and grow just as any other human being would.

A young girl named Mary is chosen to give birth to Jesus. The angel Gabriel appears to explain to her what is going on. She is quite confused, because she is a virgin. But Gabriel assures her that "nothing is impossible with God" (Luke 1:37). An angel also has to appear to Joseph, because when Mary turns up pregnant, he is about to "divorce" her quietly. (Although Mary and Joseph were only engaged at the time, engagements then were much more binding than are those today.) Both Mary and Joseph do as instructed and await the birth of Jesus without having any sexual contact in the meantime (Matthew 1:24–25).

The Bible does not support many of our Christmas traditions. We do know that Mary and Joseph left Nazareth to go to Bethlehem because of a Roman-ordered census. (No doubt they were glad to get out of town during the final stage of her pregnancy to avoid local gossip.) And we know that when Jesus was born, Mary and Joseph laid him in a manger. But we don't know that he was in a stable; it might have been a cave. (All we do know is that the inn was full.) We know shepherds visited him, as well as magi from the East. But when the wise men got there, Jesus was in a house, so they weren't likely kneeling around the manger with the shepherds. We aren't told how many wise men came, only that they presented the child with three gifts.

Yet it seems clear that God was alerting certain segments of the world that something earthshaking was taking place. An army of angels fills the sky to direct the shepherds to the manger. A star points the way for the magi. And when Jesus' parents present him at the temple, two people separately approach them with prophecies about what the child will do (Luke 2:25–38).

The Bible says little about Jesus' childhood, but the few clues we have indicate that he was an extraordinary person. Even at the age of twelve, he was able to hold the attention of the religious leaders in the temple, causing all who hear him to be amazed (Luke 2:41–52).

Jesus' Baptism and Temptation
(MATTHEW 3:1–4:11)

The prophet Malachi had told the world to watch for the prophet Elijah to appear "before that great and dreadful day of the LORD comes" (Malachi 4:5). Isaiah had predicted a voice in the desert calling, "Prepare the way for the LORD" (Isaiah 40:3). Jesus would later identify this "Elijah" as John the Baptist (Matthew

11:11–15), who prepared the way for Jesus by preaching in the desert, calling people to repentance, and alerting them that "the kingdom of heaven is near" (Matthew 3:1–2).

We next see Jesus at age thirty, coming to John to be baptized. John is reluctant at first but does as Jesus asks. As Jesus comes up out of the water, the Spirit of God descends like a dove. "And a voice from heaven said, 'This is my Son, whom I love; with him I am well pleased'" (Matthew 3:16–17).

Jesus is then led by the Spirit into the wilderness, where he fasts for forty days and is tempted. Three times Satan tries to persuade Jesus to do something wrong or self-centered, and each time Jesus responds with an appropriate quote from the Old Testament that rebuffs Satan.

Jesus' Relationships

Jesus' nontraditional yet authoritative teaching style quickly attracts followers. He spends a night in prayer (Luke 6:12–16) and then chooses twelve of his followers to be apostles (specially commissioned disciples). Among the twelve are some who had been disciples of John the Baptist. Jesus then begins to reiterate John's message: "Repent, for the kingdom of heaven is near" (Matthew 4:17).

The twelve apostles are Simon (whom Jesus named Peter); Andrew; James; John; Philip; Bartholomew (Nathanael); Matthew (Levi); Thomas; James (the son of Alphaeus); Simon the Zealot; Thaddaeus (also identified as Judas, son of James); and Judas Iscariot.

Over his three-year ministry, Jesus develops a bond with this circle of friends. He is especially close to Peter, James, and John, who accompany him at times when the others aren't around—such as at his Transfiguration (more on this in chapter 10) and in the Garden of Gethsemane just before his arrest.

But what the Bible reveals about Jesus' relationships is frequently surprising. He is usually at odds with the religious leaders of his day (particularly the Pharisees and Sadducees). But when a Pharisee named Nicodemus comes to see him one night, he and Jesus have a fascinating conversation (John 3).

Zacchaeus, a despised tax collector, changes his cheating ways after a single dinner with Jesus (Luke 19:1–10). Jews and Gentiles alike are amazed at Jesus' willingness to help and heal them.

Jesus has great respect for women. Several follow him in his travels. Mary and Martha are close friends. The Samaritan woman at the well (John 4) is stunned that any man would even speak to her, yet her conversation with Jesus initiates a spiritual revival in her village. A woman caught in the act of adultery is brought to Jesus, primarily to force him to pass judgment on her. He refuses to condemn her, yet he cautions her to "go now and leave your life of sin" (John 8:1–11).

Even little children receive the comfort and compassion of Jesus. The disciples try to keep the kids out of the way, but Jesus scolds the adults and says, "The kingdom of heaven belongs to such as these" (Matthew 19:13–14). The self-proclaimed "experts" don't get much respect from Jesus, but those with childlike faith are always welcome.

Jesus' Emotions

The humanity of Jesus is also reflected in his wide range of emotions. He weeps at the death of his friend Lazarus (John 11:35). He gets angry and distressed when people use religious law in an attempt to trap him and disregard humanity as they do (Mark 3:1–6). His anger grows into righteous indignation on at least one occasion: he makes a whip and drives animals and money changers from the temple (John 2:12–17).

But mostly, he seems to enjoy life and appreciate people. Numerous times we read of his compassion going out to a person or group. And apparently Jesus attends so many parties with "sinners" that the religious authorities accuse him of being "a glutton and a drunkard" (Matthew 11:18–19).

According to the Bible, Jesus' humanity serves many purposes. Because he shared every human weakness and temptation that we do, he is well qualified to serve as our "high priest" and give us access to God (Hebrews 4:14–16). He understands our pain when we suffer (Philippians 3:7–10). But most of all, as we look at Jesus, we see what God is like. He is not just a list of rules and laws. He isn't a condemning and vengeful thunderbolt thrower. The love and compassion Christ shows to people reflect God's feelings for us.

Because of Jesus' humanity, "anyone who has seen me has seen the Father" (John 14:9).

Jesus

His Teachings

People have a vast number of opinions about Jesus: whether or not he was God, whether or not he actually died and came back to life, and to what degree he was superior to other prophets and religious leaders. But almost everyone agrees that he was an exceptional teacher. So let's look briefly at a number of things he taught.

The Sermon on the Mount (MATTHEW 5–7)

Jesus' Sermon on the Mount presents a phenomenally different way to approach life. Jesus affirms: "Do not think that I have come to abolish the Law or the Prophets; I have not come to abolish them but to fulfill them" (Matthew 5:17). Yet his interpretation of the Scriptures and the challenges he puts forth are different from anything people have ever heard.

He begins with the Beatitudes—statements of blessedness (see pages 99–100). He teaches that people are blessed who are poor in spirit ... mournful ... meek ... merciful ... pure in heart ... peacemakers ... who hunger and thirst for righteousness ... and who are persecuted because of that righteousness (Matthew 5:3–10). Followers of God, he said, are like the salt of the earth and the light of the world, and they should be a positive influence on those around them.

Jesus teaches that murder begins with anger, and adultery with lust. And he discourages any further hatred of enemies, calling on his listeners to love their enemies instead.

It is in the Sermon on the Mount that we find the Lord's Prayer (Matthew 6:9–13) (see pages 100–101). In addition, our faith should negate much worry, and our concern should be more for storing "treasures in heaven" than for the accumulation of possessions (Matthew 6:20).

Jesus instructs us not to judge others, yet he also says to watch out for false prophets who "come to you in sheep's clothing, but inwardly they are ferocious wolves" (Matthew 7:15). And he says that those who are wise will listen to what he says and be like one who builds his house (life) on rock rather than sand.

Jesus' Parables

Although the Sermon on the Mount is clear and simple to understand (if not to apply), Jesus also uses parables in his teaching. His parables are simple stories that carry a weighty religious meaning for those with the faith to understand (Mark 4:10–12, 33–34). Those without spiritual discernment will be unable to understand to the same degree as believers.

Jesus' parables refer to things that are common in first-century Israel: seeds, fishing nets, sheep, fig trees, and such. The most popular parables seem to pertain to relationships. Two of his best-known parables are the stories of the prodigal son (Luke 15:11–32) and the good Samaritan (Luke 10:30–37).

Even in the parable format, it's hard to miss the main points of these stories: a fresh perspective of God as a compassionate, forgiving father, and a higher standard for how we should interact with one another. These two parables emphasize what Jesus says are the greatest commandments of all: to love God wholeheartedly, and to love one's neighbor as oneself (Matthew 22:34–40).

Jesus versus the Religious Authorities

Reading through the Gospels, we see that sometimes Jesus can be downright confrontational. Many of his teachings are unabashedly bold. He calls his disciples to a deeper commitment to him—above family and everything else (Luke 9:57–62). He is clear that following him will require "taking up a cross" (Matthew 10:37–39). He speaks of suffering and death as common expectations (Matthew 10:17–20, 28). And at times his frank, uncompromising teachings cause many potential followers to walk away.

But perhaps his boldest statements are reserved for the religious leaders who continually oppose him. If Jesus heals someone on the Sabbath, they overlook the fact that a suffering person is no longer in pain. Rather, they accuse Jesus of "working" on the Sabbath—an infraction of their law. Time after time they set up situations to try to trap him. But Jesus always sees through their sneakiness and puts them in their place.

It has gotten to the point where the law, as interpreted and applied by the religious leaders, seems little more than a long list of rules and regulations. The aspect of developing a relationship with God has been downplayed to the point of nonexistence. One time Jesus even berates the Pharisees with a long series of "woes," listing their offenses and calling them "blind guides," "hypocrites," "snakes," and a "brood of vipers" (Matthew 23). Whenever Jesus sees people in authority leading others to sin or twisting God's truth for their own advantage, he calls them on it. Once he has a young child come forward and says, "If anyone causes one of these little ones who believe in me to sin, it would be better for him to have a large millstone hung around his neck and to be drowned in the depths of the sea" (Matthew 18:1–6).

Some people dwell primarily on the harsh or difficult sayings of Jesus, and they reach inaccurate, perhaps even twisted, opinions about him. But taken as a whole, Jesus' teachings are a fascinating body of work, calling his listeners to a more involved life and assuring them that rewards are in store for those who devote themselves to God.

TEN

Jesus

His Divinity

If Jesus had done little more than spend his three public years of ministry teaching and relating to people, he still would probably be one of the most-talked-about figures in history. His outlook on life, his unbridled compassion for the losers of society, and his nonviolent yet direct confrontations with pompous or misguided religious authorities are enough to seal his place in the history books. But the Bible records many other things he did—things to indicate he is more than just a quirky and well-regarded human being. If Jesus' claims are true, he is indeed God.

Jesus' Miracles

The power of God is evident through Jesus' miracles. Nothing seems beyond his ability. His first miracle is changing water to wine—the best wine—at a wedding ceremony (John 2:1–11). He heals all manner of diseases: blindness, deafness, blood and other internal disorders, leprosy, withered hands, lameness, and more. He casts out demons that have powerful control over people.

He can heal with a touch. He can heal by spitting into the dirt and making a mud poultice (John 9:1–7). At times his healing doesn't require any contact at all. This is the case with the paralyzed servant of a Roman centurion. The servant is suffering terribly, and Jesus volunteers to go heal him, but the centurion asks Jesus to just "say the word, and my servant will be healed." Jesus is amazed at the man's faith and does as he has been asked. The servant is healed even though he is at a distance (Matthew 8:5–13).

Another time a woman who has been ill for twelve years approaches Jesus from behind as he walks by and touches the edge of his cloak, believing that she will be healed. She is, but Jesus realizes what has happened and stops to acknowledge her faith (Luke 8:43–48).

Jesus can instantly still a raging storm with a curt command (Mark 4:35–41). He can walk on water and even inspires one of his disciples to do so on one occasion (Matthew 14:22–33). At least twice he feeds thousands of people with an amount of food that should feed only one or two (Matthew 14:13–21, 15:29–38). Nothing seems beyond his range of power: Not disease. Not nature. Not the spiritual world. Not even death.

The Bible provides accounts of three dead people who come back to life at Jesus' command. Two are described with little commentary: the son of a widow in the town of Nain (Luke 7:11–17) and the daughter of Jairus (Luke 8:41–42, 49–56). The third resurrection is a bit more detailed. Jesus is called to attend to Lazarus, who is very ill. But rather than rush to his friend's side, he waits awhile. By the time Jesus arrives, Lazarus has been dead for four days. When Jesus calls for Lazarus to arise from his grave, "the dead man came out, his hands and feet wrapped with strips of linen, and a cloth around his face" (John 11:44).

Jesus' Bold Claims

Jesus' power demonstrates the power of God, and in addition he makes a number of clear statements to confirm it. Early in his ministry, Jesus frequently heals someone and then asks the person not to let anyone know (a request that the person rarely honors). But later, as he senses the time of his death approaching, he grows bolder in his statements—most often to his disciples, but occasionally to a wider group.

Among other statements, Jesus refers to himself as the "bread of life" (John 6:35), the "light of the world" (John 8:12), and the "good shepherd [who] lays down his life for the sheep" (John 10:11–12). He says, "I tell you the truth, before Abraham was born, I am!" (John 8:58). And just before his arrest and death, he tells the disciples: "I am the way and the truth and the life. No one comes to the Father except through me. If you really knew me, you would know my Father as well. From now on, you do know him and have seen him. . . . Anyone who has seen me has seen the Father" (John 14:6–7, 9).

At Jesus' trial after his arrest in Gethsemane, the high priest asks him directly: "I charge you under oath by the living God: Tell us if you are the Christ, the Son of God." Jesus replies, "Yes, it is as you say. But I say to all of you: In the future you will see the Son of Man sitting at the right hand of the Mighty One and coming on the clouds of heaven" (Matthew 26:63–64).

Jesus' Transfiguration (LUKE 9:28–36)

In addition to Jesus' miracles and his outright claims to be God, three of his disciples are witness to another amazing event. Peter, James, and John are with Jesus when he is "transfigured before them" (Matthew 17:2). The biblical description is succinct but startling: "As he was praying, the appearance of his face changed, and his clothes became as bright as a flash of lightning. Two men, Moses and Elijah, appeared in glorious splendor, talking with Jesus. They spoke about his departure, which he was about to bring to fulfillment at Jerusalem" (Luke 9:29–31). A voice from heaven is also heard: "This is my Son, whom I have chosen; listen to him" (Luke 9:35).

Jesus' Death and Resurrection

But the most convincing proof of Jesus' claims to be God, in addition to the miracles he performs, and in addition to the astounding events witnessed by those closest to him, is his own resurrection. After being sold out to the authorities by Judas Iscariot for thirty pieces of silver and betrayed by a kiss, Jesus is arrested. He undergoes a quick series of trials and is convicted of blasphemy: claiming to be God (Matthew 26:57–66). He is beaten, slapped, and spat on. A crown of thorns is shoved onto his head. The Roman governor, Pontius Pilate, is reluctant to convict him but finally gives in to the pressure of the crowds.

Jesus is made to carry his own cross to Golgotha (Calvary), "The Place of the Skull." He is then nailed to that cross and hangs, naked, while soldiers gamble for his clothing—all that he owns. From the cross Jesus forgives his tormentors, promises a fellow crucifixion victim a home in paradise, and cries out to God.

Crucifixion was a horrendous way to die. It was intended to be a slow and torturous death, sometimes taking days. But within a few hours of being nailed to the cross, Jesus dies. A spear is thrust into his side to ensure that he is dead.

The Romans and the Jewish religious authorities hope that will be the end of things. But they know Jesus had said he would rise on the third day after his death, so they roll a large stone over his grave, seal it, and post a guard.

Yet three days later, when a group of women arrive to anoint Jesus' body, they find the stone moved and the grave empty. A radiant angel had appeared during the night, rolled back the stone, and sat on it. The courageous soldiers of the Roman Empire are "so afraid of him that they shook and became like dead men" (Matthew 28:4). (The guards apparently fled, but the Jewish religious authorities later bribed them to say that they had dozed off and the disciples had stolen the body—Matthew 28:11–15. They also promised to keep the soldiers out of trouble with their superiors, as Rome wouldn't tolerate soldiers sleeping on their posts.)

The angel is still present when the women come early in the morning. He tells them, "[Jesus] is not here; he has risen, just as he said" (Matthew 28:6). Shortly afterward, Mary Magdalene has an encounter with Jesus himself, the first of about a dozen of his postresurrection appearances (John 20:10–18). And one of those appearances is to a group of about five hundred people (1 Corinthians 15:3–8).

The Bible provides convincing evidence of the reality of Jesus' resurrection. The absence of his body from the tomb is key. When word spread that he was alive again, all the authorities would have had to do to quash the rumors was produce the body. And it is unthinkable that the cowardly disciples could have stolen a body that was in a sealed tomb under Roman guard. Even if they could have, Scripture and history tell us that ten of the remaining eleven disciples (after Judas hanged himself) died martyrs' deaths. If they had stolen the body and contrived a resurrection hoax, it certainly wouldn't have been worth dying for.

Jesus' Ascension (ACTS 1:1–11)

One final biblical event in the life of Jesus verifies his claims to divinity. The occasional appearances of Jesus take place over a period of forty days, but on the fortieth day, he gives his disciples final instructions and then "he was taken up before their very eyes, and a cloud hid him from their sight" (Acts 1:9). The disciples continue to stare into the sky until a pair of angels appears and tells them, "This same Jesus, who has been taken from you into heaven, will come back in the same way you have seen him go into heaven" (Acts 1:11).

Many people, of course, dispute any suggestion that Jesus was more than a skilled teacher. But the Bible allows no alternative other than that he was Emmanuel ("God with us"), the promised Messiah and Savior of the world. Most of the rest of the Bible will attempt to explain and make sense of this concept.

ELEVEN

The Early Church

Among Jesus' final words to his disciples was a promise: "Do not leave Jerusalem, but wait for the gift my father promised. . . . But you will receive power when the Holy Spirit comes on you; and you will be my witnesses in Jerusalem, and in all Judea and Samaria, and to the ends of the earth" (Acts 1:4, 8). The work of the Holy Spirit and the witness of Jesus' followers is what fills the rest of the Bible, from Acts to Revelation.

Tongues of Fire (ACTS 2)

Many political and religious movements throughout history have crumbled when the leader quit, died, or otherwise stopped providing motivation and leadership. At this time the believers in Jesus number only 120 (Acts 1:15), and with their leader gone, it might be anticipated that Christianity will never come to fruition.

Yet Jesus is replaced with another God-sent leader: the Holy Spirit. One day when the believers are together, the sound of a violent wind fills the room and what looks like tongues of fire rest on each person. At that point, "all of them were filled with the Holy Spirit and began to speak in other tongues as the Spirit enabled them" (Acts 2:4).

Visiting Jerusalem at the time are "God-fearing Jews from every nation under heaven" (Acts 2:5). As it turns out, the followers of Jesus are "declaring the wonders of God" in the languages of all those people (Acts 2:11). Everyone hears about Jesus in his or her own language. Naturally, some people chalk up this unconventional event to the disciples' having too much wine. But Peter assures the crowds that is not the case. After his short sermon, "about three thousand were added to their number that day" (Acts 2:41). The believers begin a communal lifestyle, eating and worshiping together, and sharing their possessions with those who are in need. And their numbers continue to grow.

Spirit-Powered People

The Holy Spirit continues to make his presence known. Empowered by the Spirit, the once-timid and unsure disciples begin to stand strong and defend their beliefs when opposed. In addition, they are given great power for healing. Jesus had once told them, "Anyone who has faith in me will do what I have been doing. He will do even greater things than these, because I am going to the Father" (John 14:12).

Peter, for example, heals a crippled beggar (Acts 3:1–10), stands up to the Sanhedrin (a sort of religious Supreme Court), has a vision that convinces him to include Gentiles as believers (Acts 10), and experiences a miraculous release from prison (Acts 12:1–19). It gets to the point where people bring sick friends and relatives into the street on mats, hoping that Peter's shadow will fall on them (Acts 5:15–16).

As the number of believers grows, the original apostles keep teaching and preaching as they bring on new leaders (deacons) to attend to the needs of the people. And even those deacons are empowered by the Holy Spirit to do great things. One of them, Philip, follows the prompting of the Spirit into the desert, where he finds an Ethiopian struggling to understand a passage in Isaiah. Philip helps the man understand and believe what he was reading and perhaps introduces the gospel to Africa by doing so.

Another deacon is Stephen, "a man full of God's grace and power" who does "great wonders and miraculous signs among the people" (Acts 6:8). He is so influential that those who oppose him provide false witnesses, arrest him, and have him stoned to death. Even then, Stephen delivers a powerful final statement about Jesus, telling the hostile crowd, "I see heaven open and the Son of Man standing at the right hand of God" (Acts 7:56). As the stones strike him, Stephen prays for forgiveness for his attackers.

Persecution from Without

Attending the stoning of Stephen (and giving his approval) is a young man named Saul, who will become the apostle Paul. But first he will become an active opponent of the spread of the new Jesus-based religion. Eventually Jesus' followers are called Christians, although this may have started out as a derogatory term (Acts 11:26).

Saul isn't the only persecutor of the believers. They are beset by opposition from numerous sources. Many experience beatings and imprisonment. James, one of Jesus' inner circle of disciples, is beheaded by Herod, who sees that "this pleased the Jews" (Acts 12:3). But Herod soon learns that he isn't in total control, as he had thought. When a group of people praise him as a god and he doesn't correct them, immediately "an angel of the Lord struck him down, and he was eaten by worms and died" (Acts 12:21–23). But his death does nothing to reduce the persecution felt by the Christians.

Problems from Within

As might be expected with any rapidly growing movement, there is no guarantee that all members of the early church are as committed as they should be. For example, one couple sell some property and say they have donated the entire proceeds to the church, when in fact they keep some of the money for themselves. It is certainly their prerogative to donate only a portion, but their intentional and surreptitious cover-up is exposed as lying to God (Acts 5:4).

Confronted by Peter, the husband drops dead where he stands. Three hours later, unaware of what has happened to her husband, the wife also insists that they have given the church everything they received from the sale of their property. She, too, dies immediately. This was a clear example that "nothing in all creation is hidden from God's sight. Everything is uncovered and laid bare before the eyes of him to whom we must give account" (Hebrews 4:13). And as a result, "great fear seized the whole church and all who heard about these events" (Acts 5:1–10).

Another man, a sorcerer, sees the power of the Holy Spirit at work and offers the disciples money to receive it. He is severely rebuked (Acts 8:9–25). Yet another sorcerer tries to oppose Paul (after his remarkable conversion) and is blinded for a length of time (Acts 13:4–12).

As time passes, various doctrines and teachings begin to drift into the church that aren't completely grounded in truth. Some of those problems will become more damaging to the church than the external persecution. Yet the Holy Spirit working through Jesus' committed followers provides power and wisdom for the early church to continue to persevere and grow.

TWELVE

Paul

His Life and Ministry

Other than Jesus, Paul is perhaps the most significant figure in the New Testament. Although Peter, John, and other of Jesus' disciples went on to have influential and lasting ministries, Paul took the gospel of Jesus to a whole new realm: the Gentile nations.

Paul's Background

In Paul's first appearance in the Bible, he isn't seen as a good guy. While Stephen is being stoned to death, Paul is watching the coats of the stone throwers and giving assent to their actions (Acts 7:57–58, 8:1). At some point his name changes from Saul to Paul, but the change isn't explained. Perhaps he took a more Gentile-sounding name when he began a ministry to those outside the Jewish faith.

But Paul is certainly a good Jewish man. He was born in Tarsus, a city rich with Greek and Roman influences. Not only was his father a Pharisee, but Paul also had the honor of being born a Roman citizen, which gave him certain privileges. And he studied under a respected rabbi named Gamaliel (Acts 22:3, 26:4–5). So when the followers of Jesus attempt to introduce new teachings to the Jews that conflict with his beliefs, Paul does all he can to arrest, imprison, and put them to death (Acts 26:9–11).

Paul's Conversion (ACTS 9:1–19, 22:1–21, 26:9–18)

One day Paul has gotten permission to go to Damascus (about 150 miles away) to seek out any believers in Jesus, planning to bring them back to Jerusalem as prisoners. But along the way, he is stopped in his tracks by a brilliant light from heaven. He falls to the ground and hears a voice ask, "Saul, Saul, why do you persecute me?" Unable to see, Paul asks, "Who are you, Lord?" The voice replies: "I am Jesus, whom you are persecuting. Now get up and go into the city, and you will be told what you must do" (Acts 9:4–6).

The men with Paul hear something but don't know what is going on. Clearly something has happened to Paul because he remains blind for three days. A brave and faithful disciple in Damascus named Ananias is instructed by God to restore Paul's sight and introduce him to the believers there. Ananias does as he is told, and Paul believes and is baptized. When the Jewish leaders discover that Paul has converted, they plot to kill him. Paul faces much persecution for the rest of his life.

Paul's Mission

After his conversion, Paul quickly becomes just as passionate to spread the word about Jesus as he had previously been to persecute believers. He realizes God has been preparing him for this transformation (Galatians 1:13–17). And indeed, the work of Paul is responsible for much of the New Testament. The book of Acts (written by Luke) records much about Paul's life and is followed by thirteen epistles (letters) written by Paul to various people and churches.

Soon he is called to travel with another disciple, Barnabas, and take the good news about Jesus to other places. This would be the first of three missionary journeys. Paul helps start churches, later revisiting or writing many of them in order to keep in touch. His teaching and instructions to the churches lay the groundwork for much of the doctrinal basis for Christianity.

Paul's Suffering

Paul considers suffering for his beliefs to be not only a reasonable expectation for a Christian but also a privilege because it connects him with the suffering of Jesus. When a group of pseudoapostles attempt to usurp his authority, he gives a succinct description of some of the things he had been through:

> I have worked much harder, been in prison more frequently, been flogged more severely, and been exposed to death again and again. Five times I received from the Jews the forty lashes minus one. Three times I was beaten with rods, once I was stoned, three times I was shipwrecked, I spent a night and a day in the open sea, I have been constantly on the move. I have been in danger from rivers, in danger from bandits, in danger from my own countrymen, in danger from Gentiles; in danger in the city, in danger in the country, in danger at sea; and in danger from false brothers. I have labored and toiled and have often gone without sleep; I have known hunger and thirst and have often gone without food; I have been cold and naked. Besides everything else, I face daily the pressure of my concern for all the churches. (2 Corinthians 11:23–28)

Paul: His Later Years

Paul didn't mind arrest and imprisonment because it enabled him to share his beliefs with influential people. Late in his life he was arrested and taken to Rome for trial, after which he was released. But apparently he was arrested again, and tradition says he was beheaded. Yet he lived his life in a state of contentment (Philippians 4:12–13) and was ready to die whenever the time came. Since he was living for his Lord, he could say with confidence, "For to me, to live is Christ and to die is gain" (Philippians 1:21).

THIRTEEN

Paul

His Letters

The first five books of the New Testament have four authors. The Gospels of Matthew and John were written by two of Jesus' original twelve apostles. Mark was authored by John Mark, a young follower of Jesus. The Gospel of Luke and book of Acts were most likely written by Luke, an educated Gentile convert and occasional traveling companion of Paul. But Paul is credited with the next thirteen books—letters to churches and friends.

The order of Paul's epistles in the Bible isn't necessarily chronological. We won't worry much about the dates here since many of them are debated among Bible scholars. We'll simply follow their order in the Bible because *what* Paul wrote is worthwhile regardless of when he wrote it.

Romans

Paul's letter to the church in Rome covers so many key doctrines that it's sometimes called the Constitution of the New Testament. Paul is frank about the widespread influence of sin—"All have sinned and fall short of the glory of God" (Romans 3:23)—as well as its consequences: "The wages of sin is death" (Romans 6:23). But he is just as clear that Jesus' atoning death makes it possible for us to experience God's forgiveness, love, and mercy. He affirms: "There is now no condemnation for those who are in Christ Jesus" (Romans 8:1). Such people are "God's children" and "heirs of God and co-heirs with Christ" (Romans 8:16–17).

1 and 2 Corinthians

The letters Paul writes to the church in Corinth are considerably more personal and intimate than his epistle to the Romans. Still, they deal with numerous practical aspects of church life: church members who flaunt blatant sin, lawsuits, marriage, spiritual gifts, propriety during the Lord's Supper, speaking in tongues, resurrection of the dead, suffering, and much more. And 1 Corinthians 13 is the "love chapter" of the Bible. All or portions of it are read at many weddings (see pages 101–102).

Galatians

The Epistle to the Galatian churches is a manifesto of freedom. Legalism is already a problem in the church, and Paul makes it abundantly clear that faith in Jesus should result in freedom, spiritual liberty, and relief from the burden of keeping a long list of legal do's and don'ts. The "fruit of the Spirit" in believers' lives is "love, joy, peace, patience, kindness, goodness, faithfulness, gentleness and self-control. Against such things there is no law" (Galatians 5:22–23).

Ephesians

During his travels, Paul spent about three years in Ephesus (Acts 20:31). Yet rather than addressing specific problems there, Paul's letter challenges his readers to remain focused on Christ and what his sacrificial death accomplished. Paul reminds them: "For it is by grace you have been saved, through faith—and this not from yourselves, it is the gift of God—not by works, so that no one can boast. For we are God's workmanship, created in Christ Jesus to do good works, which God prepared in advance for us to do" (Ephesians 2:8–10). Believers have been chosen and sealed, and in response they should live in the light of the truth, and in unity with one another. They have been given "the armor of God" to equip them to do so (Ephesians 6:10–18).

Philippians

From the confinement of prison, Paul writes the church at Philippi and challenges them to "rejoice in the Lord always. I will say it again: Rejoice!" (Philippians 4:4). The letter to the Philippians is one of the most heartening passages in the Bible. Paul encourages his readers to strive for joy, humility, thanksgiving, and unity. Paul's goal is clear: "Forgetting what is behind and straining toward what is ahead, I press on toward the goal to win the prize for which God has called me heavenward in Christ Jesus" (Philippians 3:13–14).

In addition, "Whatever is true, whatever is noble, whatever is right, whatever is pure, whatever is lovely, whatever is admirable—if anything is excellent or praiseworthy—think about such things. . . . And the God of peace will be with you" (Philippians 4:8–9).

Colossians

Paul's letter to the Colossians is another one written while he is under arrest, but with a more serious tone than the one written to the Philippians. Heresy is spreading through the church, and Paul is trying to firmly but lovingly steer the Colossians back to the truth. In doing so, he repeatedly points to the supremacy of Christ in all things.

1 and 2 Thessalonians

As believers in Thessalonia have begun to die without seeing the promised return of Jesus, those remaining naturally have questions about the afterlife. Paul assures them that "we who are still alive, who are left till the coming of the Lord, will certainly not precede those who have fallen asleep. For the Lord himself will come down from heaven, with a loud command, with the voice of the archangel and with the trumpet call of God, and the dead in Christ will rise first. After that, we who are still alive and are left will be caught up together with them in the clouds to meet the Lord in the air" (1 Thessalonians 4:15–17). Rather than being a source of confusion and consternation for believers, the matter of death and resurrection should be cause for encouragement (1 Thessalonians 4:18).

1 and 2 Timothy

Paul's final four letters are more personal. Two are sent to Timothy, a young pastor and Paul's fellow traveler on occasion. Paul challenges Timothy to remain strong and provides some ground rules for church officers. He also encourages his young protégé, telling him, "Don't let anyone look down on you because you are young, but set an example for the believers in speech, in life, in love, in faith and in purity" (1 Timothy 4:12). In addition, Paul says, "God did not give us a spirit of timidity, but a spirit of power, of love and of self-discipline" (2 Timothy 1:7).

Titus

Like Timothy, Titus is a younger associate of Paul's. And naturally, Paul covers many of the same topics with Titus that he did with Timothy.

Philemon

This is perhaps the most unusual (and shortest) of Paul's letters. Philemon is a Christian man whose slave, Onesimus, has apparently stolen something and then run away. While a fugitive, Onesimus has run into Paul, and Paul sends the runaway back with a personal appeal to Philemon: "Perhaps the reason he was separated from you for a little while was that you might have him back for good—no longer as a slave, but better than a slave, as a dear brother" (Philemon 1:15–16).

Any of Paul's letters can be a good source for Bible study—close examination and personal application. We certainly haven't done them justice in this short chapter, but be assured that Paul's first-century writings continue to inspire and influence thousands of people today.

FOURTEEN

Other New Testament Letters

As we saw in the last two chapters, the apostle Paul was a busy guy with all his missionary traveling and letter writing. But during the rapid growth of the early church, all of the church leaders stayed pretty busy. In this chapter we'll look at the writings of some of the other key figures.

Hebrews

Although much speculation has been made, no one knows for sure who wrote the letter to the Hebrews. It is a distinctive work by someone well versed in both Old Testament law and the life, death, and resurrection of Jesus. Indeed, the letter is written to those familiar with Judaism, to show how the law pointed to Jesus, and how Jesus fulfilled everything that was left incomplete in the law. For example, Jesus' sacrificial death was a "once for all" event to replace the annual sacrifices of bulls and goats (Hebrews 10:2, 10).

The writer contrasts Jesus with many of the people and things revered by his or her readers, including angels, prophets, Moses, and Aaron (the first high priest). In each case it is shown that Christ is superior. His role and significance in history are unique and inimitable. The author also provides a sort of Hall of Fame of heroes of faith (Hebrews 11), followed by a reminder that those people were faithful without ever seeing the promised result of their faith. Believers in Jesus, on the other hand, *have* seen (or read about) the Messiah that God had promised for centuries, and consequently, they should live their lives accordingly.

James

The most likely author for the book of James is one of Jesus' brothers. After Mary gave birth to Jesus while a virgin, she raised other sons and daughters, one of whom was James (Mark 6:2–3). And we know Jesus' brothers didn't believe in him at first (John 7:5).

But apparently James came around. He became a leader of the early church (Acts 15:12–21), and his book of the Bible is one of the most direct and practical—easy to read if not to put into practice. He calls for believers to endure suffering with joy by calling upon the wisdom of God. He emphasizes the importance of works (being doers of God's Word, and not just hearers) as a verification of one's faith—so much so that his writing was almost left out of the biblical canon.

James strongly identifies the tongue as a problem that can't be tamed, "a restless evil, full of deadly poison" (James 3:7–8). He also rebukes those who show preferential treatment to rich people over poor, especially in a church setting.

Finally, James reminds his readers of the brevity of life and the power of faith and prayer. Rather than boasting, we should make plans on the condition: "If it is the Lord's will" (James 4:13–17).

1 and 2 Peter

Peter, Jesus' close friend and disciple, wrote two short letters. He reflected several of the same themes already promoted by Paul, James, and other writers. He calls his readers to separate themselves spiritually from the secular world and devote themselves to holiness. Although believers live in this world, they should do so as "strangers" (1 Peter 1:17) and "chosen people, a royal priesthood, a holy nation, a people belonging to God" (1 Peter 2:9).

Suffering is a part of everyone's life, says Peter, so we shouldn't be surprised when it happens. Besides, those who "participate in the sufferings of Christ" should endure their troubles with joy and perseverance (1 Peter 4:12–19).

Since believers are surrounded by spiritual danger (1 Peter 5:8–9), they should keep things in perspective by remembering that Jesus has promised to return. What may seem like a long time to us, Peter says, is nothing in the scope of eternity. "With the Lord a day is like a thousand years, and a thousand years are like a day" (2 Peter 3:8). When it finally gets here, "the day of the Lord will come like a thief" (2 Peter 3:10). And we are to keep in mind the reason for the perceived delay: "The Lord is not slow in keeping his promise, as some understand slowness. He is patient with you, not wanting anyone to perish, but everyone to come to repentance" (2 Peter 3:9).

1 John, 2 John, and 3 John

In addition to the fourth Gospel, Jesus' disciple John is credited with writing three letters and the book of Revelation. John was never one to call himself by name. In his Gospel he refers to himself as "the apostle whom Jesus loved." And he doesn't identify himself in his letters, either, though there is a strong consensus that John was the author.

He addresses his readers as "my dear children," which not only has a spiritual significance but also reflects the fact that John was advanced in age when he wrote. According to church tradition, he was the only one of Jesus' eleven disciples (after Judas killed himself) to be spared a martyr's death.

John calls his readers to make good choices: Choose light over darkness (1 John 1:5–7). Love God rather than "the world or anything in the world" (1 John 2:15–17). Don't be self-centered and petty like Cain, but be loving and generous like Jesus (1 John 3:11–24).

John focuses on the importance of loving one another, and he isn't talking about a hearts-and-flowers kind of love. Indeed, love is the verification of one's relationship with Jesus: "We love because he first loved us. If anyone says, 'I love God,' yet hates his brother, he is a liar. For anyone who does not love his brother, whom he has seen, cannot love God, whom he has not seen. And he has given us this command: Whoever loves God must also love his brother" (1 John 4:19–21).

John's second and third letters are both very brief yet offer encouragement to believers and warnings about would-be deceivers (antichrists) at work among them.

Jude

The author of the book of Jude was likely another brother of Jesus named Judas (Matthew 13:55)—not

Judas Iscariot or the other disciple named Judas. His concern is that a heresy is beginning to spread within the church. He writes to remind his readers of the meaning of their salvation and to challenge them to remember the truth they have been taught.

So at this point in the Bible we are sixty-five books down, and one to go. But the one that's left . . . it's a doozy.

FIFTEEN

Revelation

The Big Finish

Many times when someone expresses a wish to know more about the Bible, the real desire is to better comprehend the enigmatic and apocalyptic book of Revelation. This brief chapter attempts to summarize some of the symbols and content of the book, but interpreting those symbols is another matter. In fact, Bible scholars don't even agree if the things in Revelation are yet to come or have already happened (for the most part). Those who read the book as literally as possible tend to see the events as future. Those who take a more symbolic interpretation can link many of the phenomenal events described to the Roman destruction of the Jewish temple in AD 70. Whatever your opinion, Revelation is a fascinating book to read and contemplate.

Seven Letters from John's Island Exile

(REVELATION 1–3)

While Jesus' apostle John was spared a martyr's death, he was exiled for a time on the island of Patmos. While there he had a vision of Jesus in a magnificent, glorious state (Revelation 1:12–18).

Jesus instructs John to write letters to seven churches in Asia (Revelation 2:1–3:22), each of which includes a specific reference to Jesus, an acknowledgment of what the church is doing well, problems within the church, and a promise of what will happen if the church overcomes and perseveres.

From Earth to Heaven (REVELATION 4–20)

After John records the messages to the churches, he sees a door open in heaven and hears a voice inviting him to enter. Immediately he is "in the Spirit" and has a vision of "what must take place after this" (Revelation 4:1–2). He first sees the throne of God surrounded by human elders and angelic creatures. The figure on the throne has an important scroll, but no one is worthy to open it, which causes John to weep. But then he sees "a Lamb, looking as if it had been slain," who was worthy to open the scroll (Revelation 5:6–8).

The scroll has seven seals, and as each seal is opened, John witnesses something horrific taking place on earth. At the opening of each of the first four seals, John sees a horse—each time a different color—with rider. Together these have come to be known as the four horsemen of the apocalypse, representing war, famine, conquest, and death (Revelation 6:1–8).

The seventh seal initiates a series of seven angels with trumpets, each signaling another catastrophic judgment. A "loud voice" initiates a series of "seven bowls of God's wrath" (Revelation 16:1). Among all the seals, trumpets, and bowls of wrath, John witnesses both heavenly and earthly events. He sees a great red dragon (Satan) supported by two other "beasts" (commonly referred to as the Antichrist and false prophet). The number of the beast is 666, and no one can buy or sell without the mark of the beast on his or her right hand or forehead (Revelation 13:16–18).

John also sees a great crowd of people who have been martyred, who are crying out to God for justice (Revelation 6:9–11, 7:13–17). Two witnesses with great power defy the beast and prophesy for three and a half years, after which the beast attacks and kills them. But after their bodies lie in the street for three and a half days, they come back to life, stand up, and go "up to heaven in a cloud" in full view of everyone (Revelation 11:1–12).

An enormous war breaks out at a place called Armageddon (Revelation 16:16). But while the human war is terrible in its own right, even more severe is God's judgment of people who refuse to repent. After a long series of natural disasters (undrinkable water, scorched earth, darkness, one-hundred-pound hailstones, and such), Jesus returns with a heavenly army and puts an end to the struggles (Revelation 19:11–21).

In the end, the beast, false prophet, and Satan are thrown into "the lake of burning sulfur" where "they will be tormented day and night for ever and ever." The defiant humans are also judged and thrown into the lake of fire (Revelation 20:10–15).

A Happy (and Eternal) Ending
(REVELATION 21–22)

In welcome contrast is the conclusion of the book of Revelation. John witnesses a new heaven, a new earth, and a heavenly city where God dwells and the river of life flows. And "he who overcomes will inherit all this" (Revelation 21:7). The city has streets of gold and gates made of pearl, along with numerous other precious stones. There is no need of light or a temple because God's presence serves both purposes. In this eternal city, God "will wipe every tear from their eyes. There will be no more death or mourning or crying or pain" (Revelation 21:4).

And in the final chapter of Revelation, Jesus says no less than three times, "I am coming soon." While

some may see Revelation as a threatening and wor-
risome work, its intent was to inspire the churches
and encourage believers to remain faithful no matter
what.

One thing that comes through clearly in the book
of Revelation is that God is in control of earthly mat-
ters and can step in to judge and set things right at any
time. Those who put their faith in him and live accordingly can anticipate a worry-free eternity with him. It's
a happy ending to life . . . and to this *Bible to Go*.

Appendix

The Days of Creation (GENESIS 1:1–2:3)

Day 1 God creates light and separates light from darkness, establishing day and night.

Day 2 God parts the existing waters, creating an expanse between them—the sky.

Day 3 God separates the waters from the dry ground on earth, forming land and seas. The land then begins to produce vegetation: seed-bearing plants and trees.

Day 4 God places lights in the expanse of the sky: the sun, moon, and stars. The sun and moon provide light for the earth, and altogether they serve to mark days, years, and seasons.

Day 5 God creates fish to fill the seas and birds to fill the skies. Various species are created "according to their kinds" (Genesis 1:21).

Day 6   God creates land creatures, and then humans to rule over (and name) the other animals.

Day 7   God rests. He blesses the seventh day (Sabbath) and declares it holy.

The Ten Commandments (EXODUS 20:1–13)

1. You shall have no other gods before me.

2. You shall not make for yourself an idol in the form of anything in heaven above or on the earth beneath or in the waters below.

3. You shall not misuse the name of the LORD your God.

4. Remember the Sabbath day by keeping it holy.

5. Honor your father and your mother, so that you may live long in the land the LORD your God is giving you.

6. You shall not murder.

7. You shall not commit adultery.

8. You shall not steal.

9. You shall not give false testimony against your neighbor.

10. You shall not covet . . . anything that belongs to your neighbor.

Notice that the first four commandments refer to a person's relationship with God. The remaining six deal with people's relationships with one another.

Psalm 23

The LORD is my shepherd, I shall not be in want.
He makes me lie down in green pastures,
    he leads me beside quiet waters,
    he restores my soul.
He guides me in paths of righteousness
    for his name's sake.
Even though I walk
    through the valley of the shadow of death,
I will fear no evil,
    for you are with me;
your rod and your staff,
    they comfort me.
You prepare a table before me
    in the presence of my enemies.
You anoint my head with oil;
    my cup overflows.
Surely goodness and love will follow me
    all the days of my life,
and I will dwell in the house of the LORD forever.

The Beatitudes (MATTHEW 5:3–12)

Blessed are the poor in spirit,
    for theirs is the kingdom of heaven.
Blessed are those who mourn,
    for they will be comforted.

Blessed are the meek,
for they will inherit the earth.
Blessed are those who hunger and thirst for righteousness,
for they will be filled.
Blessed are the merciful,
for they will be shown mercy.
Blessed are the pure in heart,
for they will see God.
Blessed are the peacemakers,
for they will be called sons of God.
Blessed are those who are persecuted because of righteousness,
for theirs is the kingdom of heaven.

Blessed are you when people insult you, persecute you
and falsely say all kinds of evil against you because of
me. Rejoice and be glad, because great is your reward
in heaven, for in the same way they persecuted the
prophets who were before you.

The Lord's Prayer (MATTHEW 6:9–13 KJV)

Our Father which art in heaven, Hallowed be thy name.
Thy kingdom come. Thy will be done in earth, as it is in
heaven.
Give us this day our daily bread.
And forgive us our debts, as we forgive our debtors.

And lead us not into temptation, but deliver us from evil:
For thine is the kingdom, and the power, and the glory,
*   for ever.*
Amen.

The Love Chapter (I CORINTHIANS 13)

If I speak in the tongues of men and of angels, but have not love, I am only a resounding gong or a clanging cymbal.

If I have the gift of prophecy and can fathom all mysteries and all knowledge, and if I have a faith that can move mountains, but have not love, I am nothing. If I give all I possess to the poor and surrender my body to the flames, but have not love, I gain nothing.

Love is patient, love is kind. It does not envy, it does not boast, it is not proud. It is not rude, it is not self-seeking, it is not easily angered, it keeps no record of wrongs. Love does not delight in evil but rejoices with the truth. It always protects, always trusts, always hopes, always perseveres.

Love never fails. But where there are prophecies, they will cease; where there are tongues, they will be stilled; where there is knowledge, it will pass away. For we know in part and we prophesy in part, but when perfection comes, the imperfect disappears. When I was a child, I talked like a child, I thought like a child,

I reasoned like a child. When I became a man, I put childish ways behind me. Now we see but a poor reflection as in a mirror; then we shall see face to face. Now I know in part; then I shall know fully, even as I am fully known.

And now these three remain: faith, hope and love. But the greatest of these is love.

The Books of the Bible

THE OLD TESTAMENT
Genesis
Exodus
Leviticus
Numbers
Deuteronomy
Joshua
Judges
Ruth
1 Samuel
2 Samuel
1 Kings
2 Kings
1 Chronicles
2 Chronicles
Ezra
Nehemiah
Esther
Job
Psalms
Proverbs
Ecclesiastes
Song of Songs

Isaiah
Jeremiah
Lamentations
Ezekiel
Daniel
Hosea
Joel
Amos
Obadiah
Jonah
Micah
Nahum
Habakkuk
Zephaniah
Haggai
Zechariah
Malachi

THE NEW TESTAMENT
Matthew
Mark
Luke
John

Acts
Romans
1 Corinthians
2 Corinthians
Galatians
Ephesians
Philippians
Colossians
1 Thessalonians
2 Thessalonians
1 Timothy
2 Timothy
Titus
Philemon
Hebrews
James
1 Peter
2 Peter
1 John
2 John
3 John
Jude
Revelation